walk with me.

an aunt's story

a guided journal of memories

Other Books In The "Walk With Me" Series:

A Great-Grandmother's Story
A Great-Grandfather's Story
A Grandmother's Story
A Grandfather's Story
A Mother's Story
A Father's Story
A Stepmother's Story
A Stepfather's Story
A Sister's Story

ISBN: 979-8-990971202

Introduction

This guided journal is a fantastic way to create a
one-of-a-kind keepsake for your niece or nephew!

Includes over 150 thought-provoking writing prompts
written from the perspective of your niece or nephew.
Write as though you are speaking directly to them.

Also Includes:

Four Generation Family Tree
Record the names and important dates of your grandparents,
your parents, you, your siblings, your spouse and your children.

Two Recipe Pages
Share those special recipes your family always asks for!

Two Dot Grid Pages
For drawing diagrams, floor plans, property boundaries,
room layout, etc.

Custom Prompt Pages
Each section includes a page to add
your own prompt or question.

Customize the pages with photographs, clippings,
and anything else you wish to include
to help bring your stories to life.

Family

Childhood

Teenage Years

Adulthood

Siblings

Love & Marriage

Aunt Life

More About You

Looking Back

Looking Ahead

Your Full Name

Your Date of Birth

Your Place of Birth

the date you began this journal

the person you are completing this journal for

Family

Your

Your Paternal Grandfather

B: D:

M:

Your Paternal Grandmother

B: D:

Your Father

B: D:

M:

Your Maternal Grandfather

B: D:

M:

Your Maternal Grandmother

B: D:

Your Mother

B: D:

B = Born
M = Married
D = Died

Family Tree

You

B:

Your Spouse/ Partner

B: D:

M:

Your Siblings

B: D:

B: D:

B: D:

B: D:

B: D:

B: D:

Your Children

B: D:

B: D:

B: D:

B: D:

B: D:

B: D:

Where did your name come from?
Does it have special meaning?
Were you named after a family member?

Did you have a nickname as a child?
How did you get your nickname?
What do friends and family call you now?

*Describe your mother.
What qualities come to mind
when you think of her?*

What is your favorite memory of your mother?

Describe your father.
Which characteristics stand out
the most in your mind?

What is your favorite memory of your father?

Do you feel you more closely resemble your mother or your father? In what way?

Were you able to see your grandparents often when you were young? Where did they live? What were they like?

Did your grandparents ever tell stories about their past?
What did you learn about them?

Were you able to see your great-grandparents? Where did they live? Describe them.

*Were you the oldest child, a middle child,
the youngest child, or the only child in your family?
How do you feel this has influenced your life?*

How did your family spend quality time together?

What expectations or aspirations did your family have for your future?

What do you feel was the most important lesson you learned from your parents or grandparents?

Knowing what you know now,
is there anything you wish your parents
had taught you when you were younger?

Is there anything you can tell me about our family history or heritage that I might not already know?

Add Your Own Question

Childhood

What is your earliest memory?

Describe your childhood home.
If you had more than one, describe each.
Which was your favorite, and why?

Draw a layout of your childhood home or yard.

Did you grow up in a two-parent or single-parent home, a multi-generational household, or something else? How do you feel this has impacted your life?

What occupations did your parents or guardians have? Did you see them often or were they frequently away?

Describe what a typical day was like in your childhood home.

As a child, what did you want to be when you grew up? Did anything influence this decision?

What types of chores were you expected to do? Was there a chore that you especially liked or disliked?

Did you get an allowance?
How much was it?
What did you typically spend it on?

Did your family have any birthday or holiday traditions when you were a child?
Have you carried those traditions into adulthood?

What was your favorite childhood toy, game, or activity?

Did you have any childhood illnesses or diseases or any notable medical emergencies?

Is there a frightening memory from your childhood that you still remember vividly today?

Did you have a favorite book
or bedtime story when you were a child?
If so, why was it your favorite?

Who was your idol or hero
when you were a child?
Why was this particular person your favorite?

What was your favorite meal growing up?

Who made it?

Do you still enjoy it today?

If you know the recipe, please share it.

Recipe: ______________________________

# of Servings: ______________

Ingredients:

Instructions:

Who or what do you remember fondly from your childhood?

Add Your Own Question

Teenage Years

What school did you attend during your teenage years? Did you enjoy school? Would you have preferred a different school?

What was your school dress code? Describe what you would typically wear to school.

Did you participate in school sports, clubs, or other school activities?

Describe your typical school day.

What was your favorite school subject or your favorite teacher? Why?

What school subject did you find the easiest?
What subject was the most
challenging for you?

Did you participate in a youth group or youth organization? How has this experience influenced your adult life?

What trends or fads were popular when you were young? Did you participate in those fads?

Did you have a best friend or group of friends as a teenager? What things would you do together?

What did you like to do for fun?
Did you have a favorite hangout?

What types of music did you like back then? Who are some of your favorite musicians or bands from your teenage years?

How old were you when you started dating?
Were you required to have a chaperone?
Where did you typically go on dates?

Did you have a curfew?

What time was it?

What would happen if you missed curfew?

Did you have a job when you were a teenager?
What was it? How much were you paid?
What responsibilities did you have?

At any time during your youth, did you save your money for something special? What was it? How did you earn the money for it?

Did you ever get into trouble as a teenager?
What kinds of consequences
would you face?

When you were a teenager, did you have any idea what path you wanted to take after high school? What influenced your decision?

Add Your Own Question

Adulthood

How did you feel when you ventured out to live on your own for the first time?

What is something you discovered you were unprepared for "out in the real world"?

Did you receive any education or training beyond high school? What was it? Did you earn any degrees or certifications?

What jobs have you had in your adult life?

What was your favorite job? How much were you paid? Why was it your favorite?

Can you drive a car?
Who taught you to drive?

When did you get your first car?
What kind of car was it?
How did having a car change your lifestyle?

Did you serve in the military? If so, in what branch of service? For how long? What was your rank? Where were you stationed?

What is your most memorable moment from your time in the military?

Describe your first house or apartment.
What did you do to make it a home?

Draw a layout of your first home.

What organizations or groups have you belonged to as an adult? How did you become involved in them?

When did you begin to feel you were really an adult and not just playing the part?

Add Your Own Question

Siblings

Do you have any sibling(s)?
How many? Tell me about them.

Did you usually get along with your sibling(s) when you were younger? How have your relationships evolved since then?

Did you ever share a room with your sibling(s)?

If so, what was it like?

Did you share other things like toys or clothing?

*Were you and your sibling(s) competitive?
Tell me about any sibling rivalries or
friendly competitions that stand out in your memory.*

Were there any funny stories or inside jokes between you and your sibling(s) that still make you laugh today?

How did you and your sibling(s) handle any disagreements or conflicts in your youth and later as adults?

When you and your sibling(s) get together, do your personalities or behaviors differ from how you usually act individually? If so, how?

Did you and your sibling(s)
ever team up to convince your parents
to let you go somewhere or do something special?

Did your parents have different rules, codes of conduct, or disciplinary procedures for you and your sibling(s)? How did you feel about that?

What was a challenging part of growing up with your sibling(s)?

Are there any struggles or milestones in childhood or adulthood that you and your sibling(s) have faced together?

How did you and your sibling(s) support each other during tough times or challenges in your childhood?

Has that support system changed in adulthood?
If so, how?

What is your favorite childhood memory with your sibling(s)?

How has technology affected your relationship(s) with your sibling(s)?

Tell me about any epic road trips, meaningful vacations or other travel adventures you have had with your sibling(s).

Tell me about any advice or wisdom shared with you by your sibling(s).

What lessons or values have you learned from your sibling(s)?

Add Your Own Question

Sibling Superlatives

Between you and your sibling(s), which of you is...

The most adventurous: ______________

Most likely to break the rules: ______________

Going to take the longest to get ready: ______________

The family comedian: ______________

Most likely to take a TV show WAY too seriously: ______________

Most likely to bring home a stray animal: ______________

The best cook: ______________

The most creative: ______________

Most like Mom: ______________

Most like Dad: ______________

Most concerned about appearances: ______________

Up before the sun rises (a morning person): ______________

Still up when the sun rises (a night person): ______________

Most likely to sleep through an earthquake: ______________

The biggest drama king/queen: ______________

The most likely to cry during a movie: ______________

The one who does everything at the last minute: ______________

The biggest flirt: ______________

Most likely to yell at the TV during sporting events: ______________

Most likely to take charge in an emergency: ______________

Sibling Superlatives

Between you and your sibling(s), which of you is...

The most accident prone: ____________________

Most likely to crash on your couch: ____________________

A Mommy's boy/girl: ____________________

A Daddy's boy/girl: ____________________

Always trying to save the Earth: ____________________

The most conventional: ____________________

The "free spirit": ____________________

Most likely to become famous/infamous: ____________________

The most competitive: ____________________

Most likely to always have a coffee in hand: ____________________

Always late (with no excuses): ____________________

Always early (and lets everyone know about it): ____________________

Most likely to show up when there is free food: ____________________

The beauty: ____________________

The brains: ____________________

The one always called to help with technology: ____________________

Our parents' favorite: ____________________

The best one to go to for cheering up: ____________________

The life of the party: ____________________

The first to know everything in the family: ____________________

Love &
Marriage

In your own words, tell me what love is. Has your definition of love changed through the years? If so, how?

Tell me about your first crush.
Who was it? How did you know them?
Did they know you had a crush on them?

Who was your first love?
What attracted you to this person?

How many serious personal relationships have you been in? What did you learn from them?

Tell me about the hardest breakup you've experienced. How did you heal from it?

What is the most difficult relationship challenge you have had to face? Were you able to overcome it? How?

Have you ever been married?
What made you feel you chose
the right person to be your life partner?

When and how did you meet the person you married? How old were the two of you? What was it about them that attracted you?

What is your favorite memory from your time with this person?

What did your friends and family think of the person you married?

Describe your wedding ceremony.
Who was there to celebrate with you?

Did you have a honeymoon? If so, where did you go? What do you remember most about the place?

Have you had more than one marriage?
How do you feel those relationships
differed from each other?

What advice about relationships, love and marriage can you share with me?

Add Your Own Question

Aunt Life

How did you feel when you learned you were going to be an aunt?

Tell me about the day
I came into your life.

Did you offer any child rearing advice to my parents? If so, what was it?

Did you ever disagree with my parents about how I was being raised?

What did you think of me when I was younger? How do you see me now? What do you think are my strengths and areas where I could grow?

At what point in our relationship do you feel we were the closest?

What part of our relationship do you feel was the most difficult for you?

How do you feel our relationship has changed or grown over the years?

What is a favorite memory of us together?
Is there a particular moment or experience with me
that stands out to you?

Tell me about any children you have had. Describe their personalities.

How well do feel your children get along with their cousins? Is there anything you have done to encourage and strengthen their bond?

How important do you feel
family events and holidays gatherings have been
in fostering relationships among the cousins?

How do you balance time and attention between your children and their cousins during family gatherings?

What is a special recipe you always bring to family gatherings? Tell me about it. Why is it your go-to dish?

Please share your special recipe.

Recipe:

# of Servings:

Ingredients:

Instructions:

Is there anything you've always wanted us to do together but we haven't had the chance?

Is there anything in our relationship you wish had been different? Is there anything you would like to try to change now?

Add Your Own Question

More About You

How would you describe yourself?
How do you feel others would
describe you? Why?

Is there anything about yourself that you would change if you could? What is it and why?

What hobbies do you have?
How did you become interested
in these hobbies?

Do you practice a religion? If so, is it the same religion as your parents and grandparents?

How do you feel religion has influenced your life?

Who is your best friend?
How long have you known them?
What draws you to them?

What are your "good habits"?
Do you have any "bad habits"?

Are you usually a rule follower or a rebel? Tell me about a time you did the opposite of your usual behavior.

What is something that others don't usually know about you?

What do you think your family and friends would say is the best part of you? Would you agree?

When you need to take a break for self care or me time, what things do you like to do?

Have you volunteered for any organizations? Where have you volunteered? What did you do? When and why did you start volunteering?

Have you received any special awards or recognitions in your life? What were they, and when did you receive them?

What Is Your Favorite...

Food: ____________________

Cuisine: ____________________

Dessert: ____________________

Drink: ____________________

Candy: ____________________

Game or Sport: ____________________

Athlete: ____________________

Book: ____________________

Author: ____________________

Television Show: ____________________

Movie: ____________________

Movie Genre: ____________________

Actor or Actress: ____________________

Composer: ____________________

Song: ____________________

Singer: ____________________

Music Genre: ____________________

Animal: ____________________

Vacation Destination: ____________________

What Is Your Favorite...

Pastime: ______

Modern Convenience: ______

Place to Shop: ______

Gadget or Tool: ______

Flower: ______

Person in History: ______

House Style: ______

Color: ______

Artist: ______

Article of Clothing: ______

Type of Weather: ______

Way to Relax: ______

Warm Weather Activity: ______

Cold Weather Activity: ______

Season: ______

Holiday: ______

Thing You Can't Live Without: ______

Quote or Verse: ______

______

Add Your Own Question

Looking Back

What has been your favorite age or stage in life so far? Why?

Have you traveled much?
What places have you been?
What was your favorite place to visit?

*Tell me about any pets you have had.
If you've never had a pet,
were there any you wanted?*

Tell me about your initial reaction to computers and the internet. How has the internet, e-commerce, and social media impacted your life?

What is some great advice you have received?
Who gave it to you?
How have you benefited from it?

Describe a difficult choice that you have had to make in your life. How did you reach your decision?

Tell me about a time you surprised yourself
and did something
you didn't think you could.

Regarding world events and politics, how do you feel the views of your parents and grandparents have influenced your own perspective?

Have your political views changed over time from social influences or life experiences? How? Were there any particular events that caused this change?

What social issues of today did you see during your childhood?
Do you feel things have improved?

What are the most significant differences you see between the world of your childhood and the world today?

What hardships have you experienced in your life? What challenges did you face? How did you overcome those challenges?

Can you tell me about
some defining moments in your life?

Did any historical events surprise or scare you? Did any make you hopeful for the future?

What is something you feel you would do differently if given the chance? What impact do you feel this change would have on your life?

What do you wish you had done more of in your life? What do you wish you had spent less time doing?

What do you like the most about your generation?
What do you like the least?

Do you have any unfulfilled dreams? Something you have always wanted to do but haven't?

Add Your Own Question

Looking Ahead

What are you looking forward to the most at this stage in your life?

Describe your vision of a perfect day.

What goals or dreams
are you working toward right now?

Do you have any skills or special knowledge that you would like to teach me or share with me?

What are some new skills you would like to learn?

What do you hope I learn from you and your life experiences?

Which family traditions or stories hold special meaning for you, and which ones do you wish to see continued?

What are some of the "life lessons" you have gathered along the way?

What changes in this world do you hope will occur for the benefit of future generations?

How do you want to be remembered by your family and friends?

What advice can you share with me to help me in the future?

Add Your Own Question

Made in the USA
Middletown, DE
18 September 2024

60572025R10128